WINNING SECONDS

IS YOUR TIMING RIGHT?

By

**KEN WILKINSON
(F4MU5)**

CONTENTS

DEDICATION iv

INTRODUCTION vi

CHAPTER 1
  The Clocks Always Ticking. 1

CHAPTER 2
  Every Second Counts. 9

CHAPTER 3
  Fireworks. 19

CHAPTER 4
  Being Humble. 23

CHAPTER 5
  Just Incase 33

CHAPTER 6
  The Final Seconds 45

DEDICATION

This is a dedication to Alan Turner, who gave me books of success, motivation and inspiration to read. These books provided inspirations to millions but didn't provide my type of inspiration in them. I was the only one that could change that. These books inspired me to write my own story. So here we are.

This is a dedication to life and I hope this helps many more reach their full potential. I didn't write this to change you. I wrote this to inspire you. We can all be a little better. All of this starts from the inside out.

This is the winning seconds we all need!

It's small on fluff and big on inspiration! Every second counts!

INTRODUCTION

Hello, hi, what's up, how are you doing? Yes, you. I hope great. If you're not excited yet, lets get you there.

I'm Ken Wilkinson (F4MU5), it's a pleasure to have you here. Winning seconds explains how I propelled myself to extra just in case savings. An 800+ credit score and 2 homes by the age of 35 after starting with nothing. I now have self-confidence and reliability almost anybody can relate with. Oh no! I know some of you are thinking he's one of those people that gets along with everybody. Yup, that's me! I can explain to you how I did it. It was part natural and part effort.

Did he say 2 homes? Yes, I did. Why, you're probably asking? Just because my son needs a home too. Even though he's only 7 right now, I'm planning ahead. Hopefully, you'll understand this by the time I'm finished. I know tomorrow is not promised but I'm ready for it.

I'm not an English major, please forgive me in advance. Some of the hardest lessons you learn come from the wrong angle sometimes. This will be unorthodox. I wanted to write this from my own point of view. Might be some run-on sentences if I get too excited and forget to breathe while I'm typing this. This is your only warning. I don't want you falling asleep reading this but learning should be fun.

I might have overdone it on the introduction but you can never say I didn't try. I'm excited to share such a positive story. I was going to name this a bunch of different things but winning seconds is something we all need.

Each chapter I'll cover how the rules I set for myself played a role in each decision of my life and how it changed my life towards a life of comfort. Do you want to be comfortable? Trick question... I'm sure we all do. This is my mini-documentary.

I'm going to talk like I usually talk. I'll ask a lot of questions and hopefully, you'll be able to answer them for yourself. You can stop me any time though, lucky you my friend would say. I know you can stop paying attention any time but we're almost onto something I think you can benefit from. Spare me a few seconds.

I was poorly educated but that was validated with a certificate of accomplishment. A piece of paper I couldn't sell for 5 cents. Something we all have in common. Maybe my parents would buy it

I thought. No luck there either. In all reality, it's a get a job certificate. No matter if it's high school or college. My certificate they eventually placed next to GED on job applications. Their goes that advantage.

More than half of us are bunched together with kids that dropped out halfway through and practiced for one test. While I wasted time going from class to class all day long. They got a head start on life with the chances of making it work just as well as mine. What would be the difference in making it? For some of us, it's luck and connections. For some of us, its hard work and that's where I come in.

No, I'm not a math major. No, I'm not a certified accountant either but we're going to do some life budgeting down to the second. We'll be number-crunching possibilities that can change your life unless you're awesome already. I sure hope you are. If not, you'll have more time to do so. I was just motivated enough to put the pieces together myself, I know you can do it too.

I was raised in Queens & Brooklyn, NY in the 90s. It wasn't an easy task, the American dream was a tough challenge for everyone. My parents were always working. They both had 2 jobs. They left us in the care of others most of the time if we weren't watching each other. I'm 1 out of 5 boys being second to youngest. I was born into debt but I turned that into a positive one second at a time.

This is my mini-story. I'll take you back to the very beginning and build on my winning seconds.

CHAPTER 1
The Clocks Always Ticking

Right around the time of your conception. The chances of you being here are a million to one. I guess we all got lucky huh. That hustle got us here and I'm sure you still got it in you. It was a race and every second counted. You won the most important race and now it's time to keep winning. Lucky you, you still have time to get your timing right. From now on, don't count your days. Count your seconds, it'll change you forever.

Before you're born, the countdown to your birth is estimated. Planning and saving begins. How many diapers will you need? How much will your parents need to support you and them? Can they make it if mom is off 6 weeks with no pay? Will they both work or does one person make enough for one of them to stay home? More importantly, will they still be together? Only time will tell but the clocks still ticking.

How much time do they need? How much time

will you need? Nobody knows for sure.

So many questions, so many problems, and no clear answers. Who's supposed to handle all of these questions without struggle. Throwing money at it doesn't make it easier. People with money still struggle with this every day. Please don't let money handicap you. Time is your most valuable asset.

Expected and unexpected hurdles are coming our way and we're not ready. Maybe you're not even close to ready. Most of us are seconds away from crumbling into a bad state and the clock keeps ticking. Who's watching the clock though? Only somebody looking to get off work. Nobody watches time better than these people. I know, I was one of them. Those are the longest seconds of the day somehow. It feels like an eternity. Just imagine your seconds can be like that all the time if you take advantage of them.

When you're finally born, your race to be successful begins. When will you roll, walk and so on is put under a microscope but only time will tell. How much formula do you need? How long are you going to sleep? How long do your parents need to sleep to function properly? The real answer is, nobody knows for sure but the clock is still ticking.

We all got to hurry up and figure it out. The baby won't wait until you figure it out. You got to learn on the go. Most classes don't prep you for real life. Real life is more than a class. Real life is unpredictable. Too many variables for a simple outcome. You have to become more than just one variable of you.

You got to adjust, you just added more time to your clock. Still got 8-hour shifts, still need quality time with your significant other, family and time for yourself. Some of us are stressed and don't have a kid to worry about yet. You're thinking you don't have enough time but you do. You just didn't realize it yet. We'll get there!

I knew I couldn't reason with a newborn. Nobody can, I adjusted to him. Sleep when you can, every second counts. I know some people already going, I can't sleep like that. You can and you should. If the baby sleeps for 2 hours, you should sleep for 2 hours. Take it, the clocks ticking.

The world doesn't care if you get a full night's rest or no rest. I stopped resting a long time ago. I feel like all I ever take is power naps.

A power nap? Yes! Let me break it down. An hour break at work and you're like, OMG I needed this so bad. An hour break at home and you're like that's nothing. It's the same amount of time. The only problem is, your minds not thinking right. You got to change the way you think.

What's a break worth to you? What is a break

nowadays? For most people, it's 10 minutes to an hour just staring at their phone half the time? Half communicating with the people in the room? Half communicating with the people on the phone and still trying to eat their food.

You're still thinking about the first half of the day you just got through and the second half you got left. Your mind is so divided right now you can't really focus but the clock is ticking.

I can tell you what you didn't do. You didn't spend 1 second improving you or working on your goals. You're falling behind by the second.

Some people are out here with chargers, back up battery packs, and battery-saving apps refusing to let their battery die. Looking for outlets all day but got themselves in a box. They got potential in their hands but nothing in them. We got to do better believing in ourselves.

You need more than sleep, what are you going to accomplish running at 20%? Maybe your knowledge and energy is low. Some of you won't even let your battery on your cell phone get that low. Don't run your life on E. You got to give you 100%.

I use to ask myself am I early enough. Then it changed to, what's early? I didn't set this standard, somebody set it for me and I had to adjust. I was no longer early, I was ready.

I wasted so much time thinking. All thoughts and no results. Everything works out fine in your mind. I gave up on that. I still do a lot of thinking don't get me wrong. I just know real results come after you apply yourself and I'm all about real results.

I started doing real-world testing. I failed a lot. That could have been my name. Failed a lot. I didn't consider myself a failure though after a while. I was trying everything, every chance I got. Every second counts and I knew I had to make them worth it.

I stopped waiting a whole week just to find out if something didn't work. I took advantage of my time. Hopefully, you'll do the same. Don't let time get away from you. Take advantage of the time you have.

I understood the less time I spent waiting increased my real-world results. I was no longer waiting for my life to change. I was making changes myself so my life could change. We all know things work out better on our time right? You can make sure almost everything is on your time. That's the highlight of winning seconds.

What you do during the day is a reflection of you. Don't get up for the job, get up for you. If your job doesn't motivate you. If you hate working for other people, you should create your own job or learn to live with it. You got to get up for your dreams to make them a reality. They won't come to you relaxing.

I know some of you sleeping till you're at 200%. You're sleeping half your life away! Time is money, if you're not making it you're losing it. Money is not waiting for you. Somebody else is taking that money while you rest, procrastinate and waste your time. Put money down somewhere and watch how fast somebody takes it. If you don't care about money that much. You should still value your time because that'll benefit you the most.

How well do you keep track of your time? How good are you at math? What if you're not doing as good at life because you suck at math. Now that's a real math problem you never considered. You probably count every minute but forgot about the seconds. I know some of you are probably amazing in math, you just didn't apply it into your life right. Could a few extra seconds make a difference in your life?

How much sleep do you really need? Are you sleeping to get away from life? Maybe you're so frustrated at night you have a hard time sleeping as well. You'll get better sleep when you clear your mind. All you need is a few extra seconds to yourself daily. It'll change you, all you need to do is work harder and faster for you because the clock is still ticking.

CHAPTER 2
Every Second Counts

This has to be your most important calculation. How much time do you really have? How much sleep do you really need? We have 24 hours in a day right? Now that doesn't sound like a lot just because the number sounds low.

How about 1440 minutes in a day. Does that sound Ok to you? That sounds a little better to me, but not enough to get me excited.

Now, how about 86,400 seconds in a day. That sounds like a lot to me. I know it's a lot. That's my focus every day.

You know what you could do with 86,400 seconds. That's a game-changer, that type of thinking could change your whole life. I'm telling you right now, we all get that number every day.

You're not impressed huh? Maybe you already knew that. That's fine, let's start number crunching possibilities.

You can ruin your whole life in just a second. Being a few seconds late can set you back years. I love you or I hate you is just a few seconds but it can change your life forever. A simple pause after a serious question can change your whole mood about somebody. Somebody could say or do something that changes your mood for the whole day. Don't let less than 60 seconds ruin your whole day. Bad luck happens, people are mean and sometimes they just misunderstood your feelings. You'll be mad and they won't even know why. It's up to you to use your seconds to keep your peace. Seconds matter, think about it. What was those life-changing seconds you had? How many more do you need to do better?

Are you sleeping away precious seconds? Let's say you do get your 8 hours of sleep, 7 days a week. That's 56 hours a week. You sleep away 2 days and 8 hours every week. Without counting the time you spend snoozing or the long process you take in the morning. This calculation at its lowest turns into 121 days of sleep.

You're sleeping 1/3 of the year away. Now that's only based on just your sleep as well. This is why you don't have time. I hear people say I don't have time for that, I don't have the time for this. Guess what? I believe you. Just know, you got time and you're using it to sleep, you're using it to snooze and you're using it to procrastinate.

I sleep an average of 5 hours a day. 7 days a week. That's 35 hours a week. I'm only sleeping a day and a half weekly. I have at least a 1-day advantage over you every week. I'm sleeping 75 days out of 356.

I'm 52 days ahead of you, just this year and I've been doing this a long time. Some of you just wanted an extra 5 minutes to relax this week. I'm telling you, you got the time. You just have to take advantage of it.

I wake up on my off day and work for me non-stop like I work for a job. I'll take a break after a few hours. Time is valuable and I'm on the clock for me now. I can't put that minimum wage effort on myself.

I know a lot of you do it. Waking up just like ughhh!!! I hate this job. I look like this because of my job. I feel like this because of my job. I can't because of my job. I'm telling you right now, it's not the job, it's you.

I value my life much more than what some job set for me. I present myself at my worth. I will never lower myself to the value they set on me. Are you letting your job set your value?

You shouldn't lower yourself to the value they put on you. Only you know your true worth. Don't let a number define you. Get up and start working for you. Your outlook on life will change, and then you will change.

Just imagine, you snoozed for 10 minutes, 5 days a week. That's 50 minutes in total, that's almost 1 hour a week you lose snoozing. Somebody is gaining ground on you. If you're ahead of them, maybe you're already behind and falling further and didn't know it yet.

You said you'll do it tomorrow, that's another day. You said not right now, you said I'll start next month and you said you'll start next week. Now you're probably 3 months behind this year on top of sleep. Times however many years you let your dreams wait.

I've been out working you. Somebody else has been out working you. I'm a right-now kind of guy. I get up like somebody's trying to break into my house. You're laying there trying to sleep. I'm over here fighting sleep to stay awake. We're at different levels. I'm cherishing every second daily, you have to do the same.

Could you improve your morning peace? Are you always running late? Have you tried simplifying your morning routine? This could turn into all day peace. You can wake up and have all your clothes ready. Having your lunch prepared and ready to go the night before can be life-changing as well.

Maybe you're taking too long trying to figure out what to wear in the morning but you wear the same thing all the time. We all have our favorite clothes. You don't like that shirt with those shoes. You're trying to make sure your socks match but nobody ever sees them. You don't even see your feet again until you get back home. Stop wasting your time, he's still going to sleep with you. She's going to think your funny, it's socks. What if you woke up and everything was just how you needed it every day? You can do that once you start working for you.

All my socks were the same. My clothes were ready the night before. Not only did I wake up ready. I went to sleep ready for the next day. No better feeling than having things ready for you just the way you like it. I set myself up for success in the morning the night before. What about you?

I started my off days early, I didn't waste a second. Imagine getting up early before everybody else gets up and being able to accomplish what you want when you want it done. I've been doing this for years.

I tell people, I've been awake so long my life experience compared to your life is twice as much. My 35 and your 35 is not the same. My 5 hour nights versus your 8 hours of sleep, snoozing, procrastinating and so much make a huge difference.

I wake up at 4:45 a.m. for my job every week. When I'm off, I wake up at 4:45 a.m. for me, I like to keep a good routine so I don't have to readjust.

I know you're tired on Mondays because you slept all weekend. You took naps, you put your body in sleep mode. Now you got to readjust under pressure. Most people do this every week, I didn't.

If you keep the same schedule all the time your body doesn't have to readjust. You are now streamlining your life. You'll be more efficient. You'll be more alert. That's where you want to be, on top of your game.

I start laundry 5 in the morning on my off days. When that's going, I head out to Wal-mart to get my grocery shopping done. Why so early you ask? I need every second to count.

Just imagine, no lines, everything is freshly stocked. Nobody in the isles blocking my path and no lines at the deli counter. I know what I want. I'm in and out.

I'm back in the house by 7 the latest. I know some of you are still sleeping if you can. I'm putting in another load of clothes while one dries. After that, I'm organizing and I'm cleaning.

By 9 a.m I'm finishing up laundry, cleaning and starting lunch. I would also some days have dinner ready before noon. That leaves my schedules open for the day. Now I got from noon to just around midnight to work on my goals or whatever I need.

Some people can sleep in all day long. Me on the other hand, I'm capitalizing on every single second so that leaves me the rest of the day to work on whatever I need to work on. If I wanted to spend a hour or the rest of the day with my son, I could. I could work for an hour or two on my projects. I could spend time with my significant other. I could also have some quiet time to myself and just work on me.

Would spending more time with your kids make you happy? Would spending more time on your talents make you happy? I know it did for me. I could accomplish more in half the day than some people do all weekend. I would still have time to relax and enjoy myself without worry. Just because I did all of the important stuff I needed to do at the beginning of the day. How early have you woke up to work on you?

World records can be set or broken by the second. Every second you have matters and you should treat them like they do. We all wish those magical moments lasted just a few seconds longer. I'm telling you, you can create more magical seconds once you realize how valuable those seconds are.

Nobody I know is getting time back, nobody you know is getting time back. You're not going to get that time back, you have to use your time while you got it. That's one of the most important things you can do every day when you wake up.

Life is a race, somebody out there wants the same job you want. They want the same dream car. They want the same dream house. We all know the saying, if you snooze you lose. Don't let that be you.

People do notice your time and effort. What does your timing and effort say about you? Is your co-worker sucking up or just outworking you?

Well, we all know they could be doing neither or both. Don't waste your precious seconds thinking about it. You got to work on you all day. Even when you're at work.

You got to get up and get going. Nobody knows when it's the right time. We just have to keep putting our best foot forward. Are you going to make it big tomorrow? Maybe, but that's only if you try.

You can't sit around waiting for the perfect moment, you have to make the perfect moment happen. Nothing plus nothing equals nothing. You got to start investing your seconds into you.

The only person that's holding you back is you. If you don't put value on your time nobody else will do it for you. You got to believe your time is valuable. If you don't care about your timing, why should they?

We've all been a few seconds late. Just missed the bus, we just missed the train. It happens, all we needed was a few extra seconds. Is your timing right?

You show up late, you get whatever's left. A few seconds earlier could get you a better seat. It could get you a better parking spot. It can put you in a better place in life. You have the chance to be one of those early risers every day. Don't waste your winning seconds.

Make sure you're on time for the things that matter to you. I took control of my seconds! What will you do?

CHAPTER 3
Fireworks

This will be short and glorious just like fireworks. I stayed up so long I started noticing things differently. I was becoming more aware since I was no longer living at 20%.

I told my friend this jokingly one day but it makes perfect sense. Now we use it every time we do something that's short on entertainment but high on cash. That's fireworks! Some people live for these moments. I'm cool with being cool all the time.

I'm not saying don't do these things, I'm just saying don't do it at the wrong time. You got to get your timing right. Does one single amazing moment outlast days, weeks, or months of consistency? Maybe, that's all up to the individual. I just know that the individual is not me.

I didn't want my life to be a fireworks show. Emotional ups and downs, maybe that's more enjoyable for some. The good with the bad. Rain and sun showers do equal rainbows, pretty like fireworks for a short time. You might appreciate it more. I couldn't do it, I mean I could but I wouldn't do it. Not until I had my just in cases in place.

You can still live, don't get me wrong. Just don't live at your highest for a night without a just in case. You don't have to be at your lowest either. Life is a long race, don't light all your fireworks in one night. Find the right altitude to be comfortable.

Fireworks are that Friday feeling. It's payday, it's the weekend and people blow it all in one night. Then they wake up regretting it in the morning and the rest of the week. I didn't want to do this to myself like I see so many others do.

We all have done something or bought something we thought would have been so great or exciting many times but it fizzled out too fast. Your money is gone, the moment is gone, and you don't have a decent memory or item to remember it right? What was your last fireworks show?

My co-worker, short story, would do anything to impress the boss. I mean anything. Ok ok, not that much impressing. This a safe read, not that NSFW stuff.

She claimed 125% productivity one day. 125% in my absence. Amazing right, wrong! One happy moment in a long race. Well, she thought so at the moment, considering some of the products were made the day before. They shouldn't have been counted for that day's production without some adjustments.

You know what happened next? They raised production to her new found heights. Now she wasn't happy that day at all. Her good job pat on the back turned into her nightmare. She wasn't ready. What happened after that? she struggled to get rate again on a daily basis. This led to frustration and throwing others under the bus. She didn't want to look bad alone.

What's the lesson here? Impressing people shouldn't be the most important part of your day. Especially if it's only going to be one day. You have a lot more days to go, and a lot of seconds to take advantage of. We all need a balance. Sometimes you have to jump and hope for the best. When you do, make sure you can handle the fall. Some people are jumping on their last and it cripples them. This happens so often to people without a just in case plan. Don't let that be you. Being humble can go a long way.

I understand you're trying to have a good time. I was trying to have a good life. Sometimes you have to make sacrifices for the greater good. You might have to sacrifice some people to grow as well. That's fine, as long as you don't do it like the medieval times.

Just think, when your fireworks are done, will you be ok? Did you really need that last fireworks show? Could that money go into something that makes you happy every day? Maybe something for your mental or physical health? Take the time to figure it out before your next big show. Hopefully you'll be ready to clean up a mess after the fireworks fizzle out next time. We all know somebody has to.

CHAPTER 4
Being Humble

I could have easily called this being cheap but let me explain. Ok ok... I'm cheap! Butttt let me explain, I think it's a humble thought and I'm being really smart about it. I just felt like I had a better understanding of things. My vision board was a calculator.

Being humble gave me the money to invest. I had more time now since I was counting my seconds. I started learning new things and I started applying them. I wanted to try things, even my silly ideas. That reverse robe was silly until it sold millions right. Be humble with yourself. You deserve it. That's what I did.

I started saving pennies, I would pick them up off the floor. Now I'm not telling you to pick them up. You can leave them there for me, I'll pick them up no problem. I treasure pennies like seconds. They're powerful in large numbers. On top of that, I was also learning.

You know that water dripping from the faucet that you ignored until the bill came in? Those were pennies you didn't care about. Just like not changing your oil on time, this can lead to bigger problems. Or that funny sound your car was making and now it doesn't start. You got to watch your drip. It adds up quickly, just like seconds.

I realized the potential of pennies when I started investing in penny stocks. It was a quick way to earn money but also a quick way to lose. This was only a short phase for me just exploring the many ways I could make money.

It was only the beginning but a learning curve. To play big in the stock market, I needed more funding. I went right back to the calculator. Did I need to make more or keep more? I went with both ideas. Even though I wasn't big on buying stock, it pushed me to save more than usual.

I spent too much money on things that didn't grow in value. I couldn't tell you what an asset was really. I just knew I needed to invest in my future. I needed to invest in long term comfort. Being flashy wasn't going to get me there. I started making changes people didn't see coming.

My friends were amazed I shopped at Wal-mart for clothes, thrift stores and so on. This was a, you serious right now, what are those??? kind of moment. They would have jeans and shirts for a dollar. I would buy everything in my size. Macklemore style shopping, balling on a budget. Keeping your money is the real trick to longevity. Is your good will too good for the Goodwill?

Now, Katt Williams's calls this making pimp decision, we all know new is definitely cool. Don't get me wrong, but come on. How you going to pass up 10 for 1, that's easy decision making for me. I bought everything in bulk so it always seemed like I had more. Used bulk, but still bulk. After a few washes, those new clothes look like old clothes.

I had more for less with almost everything. I'm up on jeans. 10 for 10 if I want. Shirts 10 for 10. For a while, I wore And1's, and no named shoes I called S-Dots. Plain all-white sneakers from Walmart. Those shoes were priced at $10, I could buy 5 different pairs at once and still felt like I was saving. I use to buy 1 pair for 200 average, silly me.

Honestly, by the end of the day, I was still me, no matter what I had on. People's opinions didn't mean much anymore because I had a goal in mind. There was little to no pressure from my peers. I put most of it on myself because I knew it wasn't a name brand. I just had to change the way I thought of things. I started understanding so many things better I didn't worry about it. I was in power saving mode with all my funds. I was officially saving more all across the board.

I was shopping humbly and getting so much for less. I considered cheap meals over expensive meals. To me it was savings. I could get double that if I made it myself I though. Taking the time to make yourself a healthy meal would pay for itself. Your health should always be top priority. Don't be too tired for that.

I was cutting corners now to invest in my future. I started planning for tomorrow so sacrifices had to be made. I didn't want one comfortable day. I wanted comfortable weeks and months. How many comfortable days do you want?

Just imagine every single penny you save will add up. Are your calculations right? You've been working how long? If you calculate everything you made over the years, how much do you have left? You'll be surprised how much slipped through your fingers without notice.

A $10 pay rate over a ten-year stretch would net you around $175,000. Most people don't even have 1% of that saved. This is where being humble comes in.

My favorite place that I represented was the dollar tree like I had stock invested in it. I mean I don't like everything in there but they got some good deals. I know a good deal when I see one. I'm making pimp decisions. I stacked up snacks for lunch and my day. The size of those chips versus the size of the machine for a dollar is huge. I compared the ounces in the bag versus it's worth. I'm paying attention to details. I got time for that, yes I do!

If you buy chips from the soda machine every day that's $1. Then a soda of course because it makes you thirsty, that's $2.50. Let's say you did this 5 days a week. That's $50 a month. That's $600 a year in the vending machine. Some people do this twice a day, that's an easy $1200 on light snacks a year. My snacks cost me $5 for the week. That's 250 a year. I know we all got bad habits and they all add up. What's your bad habit?

Before that, some people also stop to get coffee in the morning. I couldn't do it, I'm watching my drip, I can't do it. I need this for my investments. I created websites, sneakers, and applications that received millions of visits and installs. Sneakers didn't do so well but I learned about the industry. I also made more money than I could ever imagine sleeping. This was passive income, something I didn't know about until after I did it. There's so many things out here I didn't know and neglected to learn. Now I'm a constant work in progress trying to learn everything.

A great app I used to tell people to use was Mint because it puts everything you spend in a budget category. If you're not sure how much you're spending unknowingly, you got to start watching the drip. You'll know for sure where your hard-earned bucks are going without fail.

You'll be surprised how much money you're actually wasting or where you're wasting it. Maybe you enjoy spending it, I'm sure the millionaires do until they go broke. They let those drips ruin them. Big homes and fancy cars require high price maintenance even after their paid off. Just be humble with the things you have. You don't need a fancy car or house. If the money stops coming for 1 month can you lose everything? Do you have a backup plan? You got to be humble. You need to get your just in cases in order.

By the time I got my friend to check he was spending $700 a month in fast food and didn't notice. He did it a little at a time, that's over 7 grand a year. What are you losing? This didn't include his fancy dinners. Maybe they weren't fancy for him but it was for me. I can't spend $25 on one plate. I mean I could, but I'm humble remember. I'm at those mom and pop $10 buffets being humble. Getting more bang for my buck, that's the type of fireworks I like.

My morning routine is vitamins and a glass of water. It doesn't matter what season it is, all my mornings are the same. I usually eat around the same time every day as well to keep my body on schedule. Some days I do vary but not by much. I keep it consistent with my work schedule.

I wasn't doing this to be humble, it just felt right for me, you got to know your limits. Get to know your body better. I watched the Bill Gates documentary and they asked him what he eats for breakfast. He said nothing. I knew I wasn't alone. Breakfast is the most important meal of the day is just a great slogan somebody came up with and here we are. Learning about marketing will teach you that. Great marketing can change the world.

If you love your breakfast, have a cheaper breakfast, have a cheaper coffee. Make it yourself, you'll thank yourself later. You got to put your money to work for you. Even if it's just investing in yourself. Some of us just eat all of our money away and it's really going down the drain. Is most of your money going down the toilet bowl? If you're spending $5 on draft beers, $10 wines, and $20 on hard liquor. You're just going to flush it down the drain in a few hours. All this money you can invest in you. All you do is get better when you invest in you. Your dream could just be making you better. Work on that for yourself.

A lot of people underestimate how much saving early can save you in the long run. Why pay top price for something that might not be cool next month. Are you blowing cash to be cool?

I'm all about keeping it simple. How simple do you keep it?

Why overdo it? Who are you overdoing it for? Who benefits more? This all goes back to timing. I wish I had somebody to pull me to the side earlier in life when I was spending 250 on new sneakers.

Expensive apparel, matching hats, name brand socks and designer jackets. I thought I was on top of the world. I thought I had a lot but that was my perspective on life. This all changed once I moved out of the box I was trapped in. I walked into a whole new world. My big move away from everything I ever knew.

In a small town outside of St. Louis Missouri. I started to put the pieces together. I moved halfway across the US. From the East coast to the midwest. No family around, no fall back plan. I had to get it right.

All I had in mind was moving forward. I used a calculator like it was a life guide. Everything I could add, multiply, divide or subtract I added to my list.

My friends partied, I saved enough to lend them money until they paid me back the next pay day. Just so they could borrow it again. We all had the same job but different goals. They thought they had everything they needed to be happy every weekend only. One pay check. Not me, I had to be ready.

Besides them, some of the locals owned land, animals, crops, boats, RVs, ATVs and they felt poor.

Huh? Are they serious, I was thinking, all I have is a few pairs of Jordan's and I thought I was doing good. That was my highlight on life. What they had to me sounded amazing. They have land and way more stuff that I couldn't ever own in the big city. Surprisingly though for them, this still wasn't enough.

All that did was just make me more humble. Rich or poor, it doesn't matter what you have if you don't appreciate it. The value doesn't come from the things you have, it comes from the value you have in you. This would make you appreciate the things around you more. This is why working on you is more important than anything. However, that's just my humble thought. What do you think?

CHAPTER 5
Just Incase

Just in case was my best idea. I'm not sure where I should've put it in this. This is one of the most important decisions I ever made.

This is my rainy days saving. I know you're jumping the gun like ok, I got that, but do you?

To the level that I took it, I know it changed everything for me.

I always had a just in case and it proved to be very beneficial because I will only do things if I didn't have to worry after.

It started off with a little, then it changed into a lot of things. One day wasn't good enough, one week wasn't good enough, and 1 month wasn't good enough.

I saved until I had 3 months of savings. I'm talking rent, car, food, bills, appliances and whatever else could set me back if I stopped working right now. I wouldn't go below this for anything.

This was my insurance, what if I woke up and my car didn't work. Who was my just in case? Whose your just in case? What if my job is gone tomorrow? Where will I work? Will I still be able to afford everything I have? Where will I stay? Would I be able to keep my place? Could I make it on my own if I came home and my significant other was gone? Could I still make it here alone? Can you handle a break up, mentally or financially? Do you have life insurance? Are you ready for some bad luck?

These are questions I asked myself. You probably asked yourself some of the same questions and just believed it would never happen to you. Biggest mistake for some people, I couldn't take that chance. I had to be ready just in case. Life is unpredictable. I didn't live in fear. I lived knowing things could go wrong and I had to plan for them.

You will lose things, you will miss moments, and you will lose people. You have to be able to pull yourself together. Others can help you but at the end of the day, it's all up to your mental health. Take advantage of your time to make that better. Work on your insecurities and your flaws. You don't have to be perfect, you just have to be happy with yourself. Don't wish you had more time after it's too late. Take advantage of it now.

Using my just in case plan prevented me from

many setbacks. It was a great feeling to have. People would always ask, what are you smiling for? The simple answer should have been, "It's a good day to have a good day". My usual answer is always, "I'm just chilling". I was happy about life, I'm happy with me, and most importantly I was just happy to be alive.

Behind the scenes, I was pushing myself twice as hard and saving twice as much. Even with all of that, my just in case was only at 50%. Life isn't all about money. I knew this, we all know this. I needed to do better. Money doesn't make you happy is a well known saying. I'm sure for some it does help and I'm happy for them.

Still, we see people falling apart all the time, they could be broke or filthy rich. Still looking for that missing piece. Some lack self-confidence. Some lack awareness. I set out to change this within myself. I started working on my weaknesses, one by one. Have you done that yet?

I didn't depend on anybody and I didn't have anybody to depend on. If I made plans, I took yes as a maybe and everything else as a no. We all have our own problems, I would feel bad pulling somebody down with me. At the same time, waiting for somebody to be there for me was a waste of time. I knew nobody was coming. Plans change and people change. I knew I had to be ready just in case.

I took my seconds and learned how to cook. I practiced cooking on my off days. 1 meal a day, 3 days a week until I figured out what I like and didn't like. I thought what if nobodies here to feed me. I should know these things. Some people are well into their 30's and still can't cook. Do you know how to cook?

I took my seconds and learned how to do my taxes. The easiest way is just giving them the money and you won't go to jail. The best thing to do is keeping your receipts for everything. I mean everything, deductibles go a long way. I sat down with my tax advisor 3600 seconds every day for a week. I knew talking to real people was better than Google. I did this every chance I got. My best advice still came from the young lady working human resources at my job. She gave me an itemized deductible spreadsheet I could use to keep track of all of my expenses for the year. This is something great to have for small businesses. You know you have to watch that drip. Do you know how to do your taxes?

I took my seconds and I worked on my timing. I started doing cardio. This in return gave me more energy. Since I had more energy I could do things faster. I bought a mini-cycle as well, so even when I was not able to run outside I was exercising sitting in the house. It fits under my computer desk or right in front of me watching TV. I limited my social media time so I wasn't so distracted. I had a 1 hour a day limit. After this, I had to do something productive. Learning something or trying something. It didn't matter what it was, as long as I was learning something new. I did this every day.

I took my seconds, studied people and myself. Now I'm not saying YouTube is the best place but theirs thousands of videos on how to present yourself. How to interact with others. How to read people, body language and more. Most of us deal with people every day. Knowing how to identify different character traits can make understanding people easier. If you understood their point of view you could get along with them a little better. This doesn't mean you'll like everybody. This just means you'll have a better understanding of the people surrounding you. You could even learn something about yourself you didn't realize. Are you a people's person or do you need to learn?

Maybe they just don't understand you, but most importantly, you probably don't understand them. Some people don't understand themselves. They go I'm so mad I can't even stand myself right now. Are you like that? Who do you know like that? Could they use a few extra seconds to themselves?

I took my seconds and learned how to budget every penny like an accountant. This came with me just being humble. I didn't want my life to just fizzle out. I kept track of everything. I was my only personal bookkeeper. Once I had a system down it was easy. The most important step is just setting it up. After that, all you have to do is keep track. Are you keeping track of your financing?

I used my seconds to improve my days. What's giving me trouble? How can I fix it? How can I learn to live with it? How can I make my day easier? I knew once I got these things out of the way, that'll take a lot of weight off my mind. I needed these gone just in case I needed to focus on something else. I needed my mind clear. Doesn't matter if it was somebody or something. I would try to fix it, make it better or forget about it. Most of the time it's just a little misunderstanding.

I worked on my health because there's no one secret for all. What I did was study myself. I ate certain foods and waited to see how it affected me. I eliminated one food at a time until I only ate stuff that made me feel better and be more productive. I googled all those weird ingredients just to learn about them. I needed to know what I was putting in my body.

I'm not really a picky eater. I understand my body has its own ecosystem. Eating everything I like would not work. I had to make healthy choices for me and this prevented me from being sick as well. I'm hardly ever sick. I know what my body likes and doesn't like. I'm no longer eating for flavor,

I'm eating for survival. You know the common cases, milk gives you diarrhea and beans make you gassy. People still do it then spend half the day in the bathroom. I avoided this after my trial and errors with various foods. Upset stomachs and hot stepping to the bathroom is a thing of the pass. Have you taken control of the way you eat?

I took my seconds and focused on stressors. We all have mounting stress we try to ignore that keeps circling back around. Let me tell you now, it's not going to go away, it's not going to fix itself. You got to fix it, or you got to learn to live with it. You got to do something soon, and the sooner the better.

I'm sure we've all had problems we put to the side thinking it was going to be difficult. When we finally got around to doing it, we were surprised how easy it was. You have a moment with yourself like, I should have done that a long time ago. That was easy! That's a great feeling to have, this will only happen when you apply yourself. You have to keep working on those little drips. Tackle them as they come and clear your mind. You'll thank yourself later.

I watched YouTube to learn so many things. Between YouTube and Google, you could learn almost anything. I learned how to fix my credit. I worked on this consistently for 2 years because I knew in the long run credit would get me further than cash if I wanted a home or wanted to start a business. By the time I managed my credit well enough to get my credit right, I no longer needed credit. It was now optional, it was no longer needed for survival with an outrageous interest rate. How is your credit score?

We all know interest rates are crazy for kids right out of high school. This is where most of us fail, right from the start. You get one job and they just start throwing credit cards at you. Hoping your hunger for adventure, fireworks and independence leads to bad spending habits. Knowing you won't be able to pay and they'll hit you with every late fee they can. Make sure your kids know better. Have you fallen for this trap?

I have friends 50k in debt. With ridiculous interest rates that'll take them forever to pay off. School debt, shopping, and partying debt. I avoided all of this and I hope you do too. School is great for some but I felt like it wasn't for me.

You could graduate at the top of your class and still fail at life. Some people spend so much time studying one craft only. It's sad to see, everything else they need to feel inner peace is missing. Especially those people that graduated and couldn't find a job after all those years. That has to be the worse feeling after so many years. You still have the time to make yourself feel better, don't give up.

You could have a huge bank account and be full of mental debt. Our lives require more balance and less overall debt. The tricky part is, overall debt is so easy to come by. I tried to avoid debt at all cost. I ended up owning a smart car after buying a German engineered car. It was high on maintenance had more miles than my original car but it looked cool. It was a bad decision but I was still learning. Now I had the cheapest car with the lowest maintenance. I kid you not, that smart car was a great decision. It was also 45 miles to the gallon, I was saving money on gas as well. I was the entertainment for weeks. Haha, Ken got a clown car, we all laughed and had a good time. Jokes on them though, I was number crunching to the penny and still improving daily.

I was becoming a jack of all trades and master of none. I made sure I knew a little bit of everything. For driving, I watched safety videos. This led to other safety training videos on various subjects. Will I ever need them, I don't know. It's better to have the knowledge and not need it, than to need it and not have it. After watching a few episodes of 1000 ways to die. Knowing a few extra things might just keep me alive a little longer. Organizing, planning, maintenance, plumbing, electrical and anything I needed to make my day easier, I studied.

I could work on my charm, my unique skills, my manners, my confidence, my patience, or anything I felt like I needed to improve on. I'm always a work in progress.

I did more than just getting to know myself. I got around to knowing my surroundings and why things work the way they do. I didn't let things frustrate me because I didn't know how they worked. I would learn why it works that way. I looked for understanding in everything. This helps with your mental peace. This keeps me in my happy place.

People think their happy place is a well-planned vacation. To me, this is just fireworks. Everything will be the same when you get back. You'll still be the same when you get back. Now one vacation is a cool idea, don't get me wrong. Take it if you need it. I saved up for 2 or 3 just in case I needed it. I realized I didn't need vacations. I just needed the option. You got so much time I hear them say. Why are you even here? I always say. I don't have time, even though they knew I was lying. Truthfully, I was ok. I'm already in a peaceful place mentally.

I didn't work when the weather was bad. This is one of the main things I use my time for. Slick roads, snow days, or ice rain. I saved my time for these. High risk and low potential. Those truck drivers never slow down, you got a life to live and that's priceless. One accident turns into a $500 deductible, some people have a $1000 deductible. I don't make that in a day. If I did, I still wouldn't go. The value of my life is worth so much more. These type of days are a hassle with the extra traffic and long delays on the road. I just avoided them. I would work all summer just to stay home on these type of days.

You need a rental car or a backup plan if you crash. You might miss work, the boss won't get you, and they'll probably think you're lying anyway. For them, it's always bad timing. On the other hand, you still got bills to pay and now you're in a jam. Your credit is bad, no good loan options and this sets you back months. On top of that, you're already behind months. You have to make sure you spare some fireworks for these days. You'll thank yourself when the day does come.

Maybe you're afraid to lose your job. Maybe you couldn't afford to lose a days' pay. Maybe you wanted to prove to your boss you were reliable, or just maybe you didn't think the weather was that bad.

Whatever your reason, make sure it's a good one. Make sure it's worth it. Some of us have kids depending on us. You can't keep risking days that'll set you back months. If you don't plan on getting ahead for you, get ahead for them. Knowing your family will be ok takes a lot of pressure off of you.

Don't let that job stress you, theirs millions of them and only one of you. You're replaceable, there's a thousand applications in there. You might be the best but the odds are against you. There's a whole world of people saying they're the best too.

We know some people got too much pride and not enough sense. Some people got the cents and not enough smarts to keep it. Some people got book-smarts and no life skills. Some people are out-going and some are shy. No matter where you are on the spectrum, it'll never hurt to work on your life balance. Otherwise, there's a good chance you'll always fall flat on your face.

My just in case took a lot of pressure off me. I was beyond independent. I didn't have to put my weight or setbacks on anybody else. I carried my weight from every angle.

What I did for my son was consider inflation after having a better understanding of how the economy works. The cost of living is always going up. I don't want him to struggle like I did. We're all working to have a nice place to live and I'm giving him a head start. He can focus on school, save or just live a humble life. If he turns out to be irresponsible I can always cash out because it's an asset. It'll be worth more later than it is now. For me, that's a good investment either way.

We all know life is cause and effect. Every day presents a new challenge. You probably can't be ready for everything but will you be ready for most of it just in case?

CHAPTER 6
The Final Seconds

Whether you wake up in the morning or you lay down at the end of the night. Do you think to yourself what is it all for? Who is it all for? Do you have kids, random stress or debt? Maybe all of the above?

But most importantly, who are you working for? Is your job setting the current tone for your life? Is it your significant other or family? No matter the cause, you have to get up for you.

How are you going to handle things when you're feeling broken inside? You wouldn't use broken tools to fix things. Start working on you and the things around you will start to change. Get your problems out of the way so you can be more efficient. You'll thank yourself later. Some of you still mad at somebody because they looked at you wrong years ago. You get upset every time you see them. You're wasting your seconds. Let it go.

I'm not showing up to work for anybody but

me. It doesn't matter who hires me, I'm working for me. I'm doing everything for me. This job is not my dream, that's somebody else dream. I'm just here working on me, for me. I can't let this job set me back. This could just be a stepping stone. Maybe you don't have dreams to chase, you just working for a living. That's ok, just realize when you walk out that door, you're working for you. That job could replace you easily.

Maybe it's your dream job, you're still working for you. For your kids, for your goals or whatever motivates you. Don't spend 40+ hours making some company better and go home and don't spend any time on you. I would be miserable too. What's your handicap, what's your motivation? How better will you be when you start working for you 40+ hours a week. Or even better, every second you get.

The clocks ticking, is your whole life depending on one thing or one person? I hope you get your just in cases in order. I hope you start believing in you. Take control of your life, your seconds and your happiness. You deserve the same dedication you give that job. For some, even better than you give the job.

Even if you didn't care about the job, you went in. When you were sick and didn't want to work, you went in. When you were tired, you went in. When you hated it, you went in. When your kids were sick, you went in. We've all done it. I just had to change my outlook.

When you go home, keep going for you. Don't be too tired to live your life. Don't be too tired for your kids, your friends, your family or significant others. If you let your whole life turn into just work, sleep and occasionally fireworks. You got to do better.

I did all of this to avoid check to check living. Life should be more than just check to check living. If you're barely living on 4 checks a month, you need to scale your life back. You need to start doing some long term calculations. They matter more than you think. My goal was to aim for living on 3 checks a month so I could save one. In some areas, this is almost impossible without great sacrifices but I believe some of you can do it.

Once you start applying the things you learn. The time you saved for you will become so valuable you'll be asking yourself, why didn't I do this sooner!? I don't regret taking time to work on my life balance. I believe you won't mind either.

I started bringing my new skills to work with me. I wasn't learning just for home, I was learning to improve my whole life. It wasn't about peace just at home, this was about peace everywhere. Being organized made me more productive at work and at home. I was no longer working in a mess. I kept my work station clean and I knew where everything was. I set up my station so I was ready to go every morning, I was a planner, I planned to make my days better every way I could.

Being at peace mentally also made focusing on my work easier as well. I also became a better representative for my family, friends, myself and the company I worked for. Just because my appearance and attitude stayed at a positive level. Uniform or no uniform, what people saw was me. No longer frustrated with the things I didn't understand. No longer worried about he said, she said. No longer tired or stressed. No longer in debt. My life was no longer just work, it was everything I wanted it to be, peaceful.

What will you do with the time you have left? What perfect moments will you create? Who will you share them with? All of this is up to you, not the value of your job.

Your daily decisions are also based on your level of intelligence. The smarter you are, the better your decisions will be as well. You see kids out here running around falling and learning. Learning from each mistake. Why did you stop falling? Why did you stop learning? Why did you stop running? Keep falling, keep learning and keep running for your goals. No matter how small or how big.

Just in case you forgot, the clock is ticking and every second counts. Don't get caught up with the fireworks and be humble in your final seconds.

www.ingramcontent.com/pod-product-compliance
Lightning Source LLC
Chambersburg PA
CBHW071506070426
42452CB00041B/2440